More Dishcloth Dresses

Enjoy the retro appeal of a dishcloth a day! Shaped as dresses for Sunday brunch through Saturday at the beach, these 7 designs are fun ways to keep your dishcloth uniquely displayed and handy to reach. Each is easy to knit using all-cotton medium weight yarn.

LEISURE ARTS, INC.
Maumelle, Arkansas

Sunday

Brunch Dress

●●○○ EASY

SHOPPING LIST

Yarn (Medium Weight) MEDIUM 4

[2.5 ounces, 120 yards (70 grams, 109 meters) per skein**]**:

- ☐ 27 yards (24.5 meters)

Knitting Needles

- ☐ Straight, size 7 (4.5 mm)

Additional Supplies

- ☐ Size G (4 mm) crochet hook

TECHNIQUES USED

- M1 ***(Figs. 3a & b, page 26)***
- K2 tog ***(Fig. 4, page 27)***
- P2 tog ***(Fig. 5, page 27)***
- SSK ***(Figs. 6a-c, page 27)***
- Slip 1 as if to **knit**, K2 tog, PSSO ***(Fig. 8, page 28)***
- Basic Crochet Stitches ***(page 30)***

SKIRT

Cast on 25 sts.

Row 1 (Right side)**:** K2, P1, (K3, P1) 5 times, K2.

Row 2: P2, K5, (P3, K5) twice, P2.

Row 3: K2, P1, (K3, P1) 5 times, K2.

Rows 4-7: Repeat Rows 2 and 3 twice.

Row 8: K3, P3, (K5, P3) twice, K3.

Row 9: K2, P1, (K3, P1) 5 times, K2.

Row 10: K3, P3, (K5, P3) twice, K3.

Rows 11 and 12: Repeat Rows 9 and 10.

Rows 13-24: Repeat Rows 1-12.

WAIST & BODICE

Row 1 (Right side)**:** K2, P1, (slip 1, K2 tog, PSSO, P1) twice, K3, P1, (slip 1, K2 tog, PSSO, P1) twice, K2: 17 sts.

Row 2: K3, (P1, K1) twice, P3, (K1, P1) twice, K3.

Row 3: K1, P2 tog, SSK 3 times, K1, K2 tog twice, P2 tog, K1: 10 sts.

Row 4: K2, P6, K2.

Row 5: K4, M1, K2, M1, K4: 12 sts.

Row 6: K1, P3, K4, P3, K1.

Row 7: K4, (M1, K4) twice: 14 sts.

Row 8: K1, P3, K6, P3, K1.

Row 9: K4, M1, K6, M1, K4: 16 sts.

Row 10: K1, P3, K8, P3, K1.

Row 11: K2 tog, K2, M1, K8, M1, K2, SSK.

Row 12: K1, P3, K8, P3, K1.

Neck Shaping

K2 tog, K3, bind off next 6 sts, K2, SSK: 4 sts **each** side.

FIRST SIDE

Row 1: K1, P3.

Row 2: K4.

Row 3: K1, P3.

Bind off all sts on First Side in **knit**.

SECOND SIDE

Row 1: With **wrong** side facing, P3, K1.

Row 2: K4.

Row 3: P3, K1.

Bind off 3 sts in **knit**; do **not** cut yarn: one st.

Slip st onto crochet hook, ch 12; with **right** side facing, join with slip st to first st on First Side, **turn**; slip st in each ch across; finish off.

Monday

Shopping Spree Dress

EASY

Shown on page 7.

SHOPPING LIST

Yarn (Medium Weight) MEDIUM 4
[2.5 ounces, 120 yards
(70 grams, 109 meters)
per skein]:

- ☐ 28 yards (25.5 meters)

Knitting Needles

- ☐ Straight, size 7 (4.5 mm)

Additional Supplies

- ☐ Size G (4 mm) crochet hook

TECHNIQUES USED

- M1 ***(Figs. 3a & b, page 26)***
- K2 tog ***(Fig. 4, page 27)***
- SSK ***(Figs. 6a-c, page 27)***
- Slip 1 as if to **knit**, K2 tog, PSSO ***(Fig. 8, page 28)***
- Basic Crochet Stitches ***(page 30)***

SKIRT

Cast on 27 sts.

Row 1 (Right side)**:** Knit across.

Row 2: K5, P1, (K3, P1) 4 times, K5.

Row 3: K2, P3, (K1, P3) 5 times, K2.

Row 4: K4, P1, K1, P1, ★ (K2, P1) twice, K1, P1; repeat from ★ once **more**, K4.

Row 5: K2, P2, K1, P1, K1, ★ (P2, K1) twice, P1, K1; repeat from ★ once **more**, P2, K2.

Row 6: K3, P1, (K1, P1) across to last 3 sts, K3.

Row 7: K2, P1, (K1, P1) across to last 2 sts, K2.

Row 8: K4, P1, K1, P1, ★ (K2, P1) twice, K1, P1; repeat from ★ once **more**, K4.

Row 9: K2, P2, K1, P1, K1, ★ (P2, K1) twice, P1, K1; repeat from ★ once **more**, P2, K2.

Row 10: K5, P1, (K3, P1) 4 times, K5.

Row 11: K2, P3, (K1, P3) 5 times, K2.

Row 12: K5, P1, (K3, P1) 4 times, K5.

Rows 13-22: Repeat Rows 3-12.

WAIST & BODICE

Row 1 (Right side)**:** K1, SSK twice, K1, SSK, K2, SSK, K3, K2 tog, K2, K2 tog, K1, K2 tog twice, K1: 19 sts.

Row 2: K3, P1, (K2, P1) 4 times, K3.

Row 3: SSK 3 times, K1, slip 1, K2 tog, PSSO, K2 tog, K1, K2 tog 3 times: 10 sts.

Row 4: K1, P3, K2, P3, K1.

Row 5: K4, M1, K2, M1, K4: 12 sts.

Row 6: K1, P3, K4, P3, K1.

Row 7: K4, (M1, K4) twice: 14 sts.

Row 8: K1, P3, K6, P3, K1.

Row 9: K4, M1, K6, M1, K4: 16 sts.

Row 10: K1, P3, K8, P3, K1.

Row 11: K2 tog, K2, M1, K8, M1, K2, SSK.

Row 12: K1, P3, K8, P3, K1.

Neck Shaping

K2 tog, K3, bind off next 6 sts, K2, SSK: 4 sts **each** side.

FIRST SIDE

Row 1: K1, P3.

Row 2: K4.

Row 3: K1, P3.

Bind off all sts on First Side in **knit**.

SECOND SIDE

Row 1: With **wrong** side facing, P3, K1.

Row 2: K4.

Row 3: P3, K1.

Bind off 3 sts in **knit**; do **not** cut yarn: one st.

Slip st onto crochet hook, ch 12; with **right** side facing, join with slip st to first st on First Side, **turn**; slip st in each ch across; finish off.

Tuesday

Lunch With Friends Dress

●●○○ EASY

SHOPPING LIST

Yarn (Medium Weight) MEDIUM 4

[2.5 ounces, 120 yards
(70 grams, 109 meters)
per skein**]**:

☐ 28 yards (25.5 meters)

Knitting Needles

☐ Straight, size 7 (4.5 mm)

Additional Supplies

☐ Size G (4 mm) crochet hook

TECHNIQUES USED

- YO *(Fig. 2, page 26)*
- M1 *(Figs. 3a & b, page 26)*
- K2 tog *(Fig. 4, page 27)*
- P2 tog *(Fig. 5, page 27)*
- SSK *(Figs. 6a-c, page 27)*
- Slip 1 as if to **knit**, K1, PSSO *(Figs. 7a & b, page 28)*
- Slip 2 tog as if to **knit**, K1, P2SSO *(Figs. 9a & b, page 29)*
- Basic Crochet Stitches *(page 30)*

SKIRT

Cast on 23 sts.

Row 1: Knit across.

Row 2 (Right side)**:** K2, (P5, K2) across.

Row 3: K1, P1, K5, (P2, K5) twice, P1, K1.

Row 4: K2, ★ P2, **[**K1, (YO, K1) 3 times**] all** in next st, P2, K2; repeat from ★ 2 times **more**: 41 sts.

Row 5: K1, P1, K2, P7, K2, (P2, K2, P7, K2) twice, P1, K1.

Row 6: K2, (P2, K7, P2, K2) across.

Row 7: K1, P1, K2, P7, K2, (P2, K2, P7, K2) twice, P1, K1.

Rows 8 and 9: Repeat Rows 6 and 7.

Row 10: K2, ★ P2, slip 1, K1, PSSO, K3, K2 tog, P2, K2; repeat from ★ 2 times **more**: 35 sts.

Row 11: K1, P1, K2, P5, K2, (P2, K2, P5, K2) twice, P1, K1.

Row 12: K2, ★ P2, slip 1, K1, PSSO, K1, K2 tog, P2, K2; repeat from ★ 2 times **more**: 29 sts.

Row 13: K1, P1, K2, P3, K2, (P2, K2, P3, K2) twice, P1, K1.

Row 14: K2, ★ P2, slip 2, K1, P2SSO, P2, K2; repeat from ★ 2 times **more**: 23 sts.

Row 15: K1, P1, K2, P1, K2, (P2, K2, P1, K2) twice, P1, K1.

Row 16: K2, (P2, K1, P2, K2) across.

Row 17: K1, P1, K2, P1, K2, (P2, K2, P1, K2) twice, P1, K1.

Rows 18-21: Repeat Rows 16 and 17 twice.

WAIST & BODICE

Row 1 (Right side)**:** K2, ★ P2tog, K1, P2tog, K2; repeat from ★ 2 times **more**: 17 sts.

Row 2: K1, P1, K1, ★ P1, K1, P2, K1; repeat from ★ once **more**, (P1, K1) twice.

Row 3: K1, SSK 3 times, P1, K1, P1, K2 tog 3 times, K1: 11 sts.

Row 4: K1, P3, K1, P1, K1, P3, K1.

Row 5: K7, M1, K4: 12 sts.

Row 6: K1, P3, K4, P3, K1.

Row 7: K4, (M1, K4) twice: 14 sts.

Row 8: K1, P3, K6, P3, K1.

Row 9: K4, M1, K6, M1, K4: 16 sts.

Row 10: K1, P3, K8, P3, K1.

Row 11: K2 tog, K2, M1, K8, M1, K2, SSK.

Row 12: K1, P3, K8, P3, K1.

Neck Shaping

K2 tog, K3, bind off next 6 sts, K2, SSK: 4 sts **each** side.

FIRST SIDE

Row 1: K1, P3.

Row 2: K4.

Row 3: K1, P3.

Bind off all sts on First Side in **knit**.

SECOND SIDE

Row 1: With **wrong** side facing, P3, K1.

Row 2: K4.

Row 3: P3, K1.

Bind off 3 sts in **knit**; do **not** cut yarn: one st.

Slip st onto crochet hook, ch 12; with **right** side facing, join with slip st to first st on First Side, **turn**; slip st in each ch across; finish off.

Wednesday

At The Museum Dress

●●○○ EASY

SHOPPING LIST

Yarn (Medium Weight) MEDIUM 4
[2.5 ounces, 120 yards
(70 grams, 109 meters)
per skein]:

☐ 26 yards (24 meters)

Knitting Needles

☐ Straight, size 7 (4.5 mm)

Additional Supplies

☐ Size G (4 mm) crochet hook

TECHNIQUES USED

- M1 ***(Figs. 3a & b, page 26)***
- K2 tog ***(Fig. 4, page 27)***
- SSK ***(Figs. 6a-c, page 27)***
- Basic Crochet Stitches ***(page 30)***

SKIRT

Cast on 28 sts.

Rows 1-5: Knit across.

Row 6: K2, P6, K 12, P6, K2.

Row 7 (Right side)**:** Knit across.

Row 8: K2, P6, K 12, P6, K2.

Rows 9-20: Repeat Rows 7 and 8, 6 times.

WAIST & BODICE

Row 1 (Right side)**:** SSK 7 times, K2 tog 7 times: 14 sts.

Row 2: K1, P3, K6, P3, P1.

Row 3: K3, SSK twice, K2 tog twice, K3: 10 sts.

Row 4: K1, P3, K2, P3, K1.

Row 5: K4, M1, K2, M1, K4: 12 sts.

Row 6: K1, P3, K4, P3, K1.

Row 7: K4, (M1, K4) twice: 14 sts.

Row 8: K1, P3, K6, P3, K1.

Row 9: K4, M1, K6, M1, K4: 16 sts.

Row 10: K1, P3, K8, P3, K1.

Row 11: K2 tog, K2, M1, K8, M1, K2, K2 tog.

Row 12: K1, P3, K8, P3, K1.

Neck Shaping

K2 tog, K3, bind off next 6 sts, K2, SSK: 4 sts **each** side.

FIRST SIDE

Row 1: K1, P3.

Row 2: K4.

Row 3: K1, P3.

Bind off all sts on First Side in **knit**.

SECOND SIDE

Row 1: With **wrong** side facing, P3, K1.

Row 2: K4.

Row 3: P3, K1.

Bind off 3 sts in **knit**; do **not** cut yarn: one st.

Slip st onto crochet hook, ch 12; with **right** side facing, join with slip st to first st on First Side, **turn**; slip st in each ch across; finish off.

Thursday

Off To The Spa Dress

●●○○ EASY

Shown on page 17.

SHOPPING LIST

Yarn (Medium Weight) MEDIUM 4
[2.5 ounces, 120 yards
(70 grams, 109 meters)
per skein]:

- ☐ 28 yards (25.5 meters)

Knitting Needles

- ☐ Straight, size 7 (4.5 mm)

Additional Supplies

- ☐ Size G (4 mm) crochet hook

TECHNIQUES USED

- Knit increase ***(Figs. 1a & b, page 26)***
- M1 ***(Figs. 3a & b, page 26)***
- K2 tog ***(Fig. 4, page 27)***
- SSK ***(Figs. 6a-c, page 27)***
- Slip 1 as if to **knit**, K1, PSSO ***(Figs. 7a & b, page 28)***
- Slip 1 as if to **knit**, K2 tog, PSSO ***(Fig. 8, page 28)***
- Basic Crochet Stitches ***(page 30)***

SKIRT

Cast on 27 sts.

Rows 1-3: K1, (P1, K1) across.

Row 4 (Right side)**:** Knit across.

Row 5: K1, P3, K1, P1, K1, (P5, K1, P1, K1) twice, P3, K1.

Repeat Rows 4 and 5 for pattern until Skirt measures approximately 4" (10 cm) from cast on edge, ending by working Row 5.

WAIST & BODICE

Row 1 (Right side)**:** K4, (slip 1, K1, PSSO) 4 times, slip 1, K2 tog, P2SSO, K2 tog 4 times, K4: 17 sts.

Row 2: K1, P7, work knit increase, P7, K1: 18 sts.

Row 3: SSK 4 times, K2, K2 tog 4 times: 10 sts.

Row 4: K1, P3, K2, P3, K1.

Row 5: K4, M1, K2, M1, K4: 12 sts.

Row 6: K1, P3, K4, P3, K1.

Row 7: K4, (M1, K4) twice: 14 sts.

Row 8: K1, P3, K6, P3, K1.

Row 9: K4, M1, K6, M1, K4: 16 sts.

Row 10: K1, P3, K8, P3, K1.

Row 11: K2 tog, K2, M1, K8, M1, K2, SSK.

Row 12: K1, P3, K8, P3, K1.

Neck Shaping

K2 tog, K3, bind off next 6 sts, K2, SSK: 4 sts **each** side.

FIRST SIDE

Row 1: K1, P3.

Row 2: K4.

Row 3: K1, P3.

Bind off all sts on First Side in **knit**.

SECOND SIDE

Row 1: With **wrong** side facing, P3, K1.

Row 2: K4.

Row 3: P3, K1.

Bind off 3 sts in **knit**; do **not** cut yarn: one st.

Slip st onto crochet hook, ch 12; with **right** side facing, join with slip st to first st on First Side, **turn**; slip st in each ch across; finish off.

Friday

Dinner Date Dress

●●○○ EASY

SHOPPING LIST

Yarn (Medium Weight) MEDIUM 4
[2.5 ounces, 120 yards
(70 grams, 109 meters)
per skein]:

- ☐ 26 yards (24 meters)

Knitting Needles

- ☐ Straight, size 7 (4.5 mm)

Additional Supplies

- ☐ Size G (4 mm) crochet hook

TECHNIQUES USED

- YO ***(Fig. 2, page 26)***
- M1 ***(Figs. 3a & b, page 26)***
- K2 tog ***(Fig. 4, page 27)***
- P2 tog ***(Fig. 5, page 27)***
- SSK ***(Figs. 6a-c, page 27)***
- Slip 2 tog as if to **knit**, K1, P2SSO ***(Figs. 9a & b, page 29)***
- Basic Crochet Stitches ***(page 30)***

SKIRT

Cast on 31 sts.

Row 1: Knit across.

Row 2 (Right side)**:** K2, YO, ★ K3, slip 2, K1, P2SSO, K3, YO; repeat from ★ 2 times **more**, K2: 29 sts.

Row 3: Knit across.

Row 4: K3, YO, K2, slip 2, K1, P2SSO, K2, YO, ★ K1, YO, K2, slip 2, K1, P2SSO, K2, YO; repeat from ★ once **more**, K3.

Row 5: K2, P1, (K7, P1) 3 times, K2.

Row 6: K4, YO, K1, slip 2, K1, P2SSO, K1, YO, ★ K3, YO, K1, slip 2, K1, P2SSO, K1, YO; repeat from ★ once **more**, K4.

Row 7: K2, P2, K5, (P3, K5) twice, P2, K2.

Row 8: K5, ★ YO, slip 2, K1, P2SSO, YO, K5; repeat from ★ 2 times **more**.

Row 9: K2, P 25, K2.

Row 10: Knit across.

Row 11: K2, P 25, K2.

Rows 12-19: Repeat Rows 10 and 11, 4 times.

WAIST & BODICE

Row 1 (Right side)**:** K2, SSK, (K1, SSK) 3 times, K3, K2 tog, (K1, K2 tog) 3 times, K2: 21 sts.

Row 2: K2, P2 tog, P2, P2 tog, P5, P2 tog, P2, P2 tog, K2: 17 sts.

Row 3: K1, SSK 3 times, K1, K2 tog 4 times, K1: 10 sts.

Row 4: K1, P3, K2, P3, K1.

Row 5: K4, M1, K2, M1, K4: 12 sts.

Row 6: K1, P3, K4, P3, K1.

Row 7: K4, (M1, K4) twice: 14 sts.

Row 8: K1, P3, K6, P3, K1.

Row 9: K4, M1, K6, M1, K4: 16 sts.

Row 10: K1, P3, K8, P3, K1.

Row 11: K2 tog, K2, M1, K8, M1, K2, SSK.

Row 12: K1, P3, K8, P3, K1.

Neck Shaping

K2 tog, K3, bind off next 6 sts in **knit**, K2, SSK: 4 sts **each** side.

FIRST SIDE

Row 1: K1, P3.

Row 2: K4.

Row 3: K1, P3.

Bind off all sts on First Side in **knit**.

SECOND SIDE

Row 1: With **wrong** side facing, P3, K1.

Row 2: K4.

Row 3: P3, K1.

Bind off 3 sts in **knit**; do **not** cut yarn: one st.

Slip st onto crochet hook, ch 12; with **right** side facing, join with slip st to first st on First Side, **turn**; slip st in each ch across; finish off.

Saturday

At The Beach Dress

●●○○ EASY

Shown on page 23.

SHOPPING LIST

Yarn (Medium Weight) MEDIUM 4

[2 ounces, 95 yards (56.7 grams, 86 meters) per skein]:

- ☐ Variegated - 20 yards (18.5 meters)

[2.5 ounces, 120 yards (70 grams, 109 meters) per skein]:

- ☐ Lime Green - 10 yards (9 meters)

Knitting Needles

- ☐ Straight, size 7 (4.5 mm)

Additional Supplies

- ☐ Size G (4 mm) crochet hook

TECHNIQUES USED

- M1 ***(Figs. 3a & b, page 26)***
- K2 tog ***(Fig. 4, page 27)***
- SSK ***(Figs. 6a-c, page 27)***
- Changing Colors ***(Fig. 10, page 29)***
- Basic Crochet Stitches ***(page 30)***

SKIRT

Wind approximately 5 yards (4.5 meters) of Lime Green into a separate ball to use beginning with Row 6.

With Variegated, cast on 28 sts.

Rows 1-5: Knit across.

Cut Variegated.

Row 6 (Right side)**:** With Lime Green, K8, drop Lime Green; with Variegated, K 12, drop Variegated; with second Lime Green, K8.

Row 7: K2, P6; with Variegated, K 12; with Lime Green, P6, K2.

Row 8: K8; with Variegated, K 12; with Lime Green, K8.

Rows 9-23: Repeat Rows 7 and 8, 7 times; then repeat Row 7 once more.

WAIST & BODICE

Row 1 (Right side)**:** SSK 4 times; with Variegated, SSK 3 times, K2 tog 3 times; with Lime Green, K2 tog 4 times: 14 sts.

Row 2: K1, P3; with Variegated, K6; with Lime Green, P3, K1.

Row 3: K3, SSK; with Variegated, SSK, K2 tog; with Lime Green, K2 tog, K3: 10 sts.

Row 4: K1, P3; with Variegated, K2; with Lime Green, P3, K1.

Row 5: K4; with Variegated, M1, K2, M1; with Lime Green, K4: 12 sts.

Row 6: K1, P3; with Variegated, K4; with Lime Green, P3, K1.

Row 7: K4; with Variegated, M1, K4, M1; with Lime Green, K4: 14 sts.

Row 8: K1, P3; with Variegated, K6; with Lime Green, P3, K1.

Row 9: K4; with Variegated, M1, K6, M1; with Lime Green, K4: 16 sts.

Row 10: K1, P3; with Variegated, K8; with Lime Green, P3, K1.

Row 11: K2 tog, K2; with Variegated, M1, K8, M1; with Lime Green, K2, SSK.

Row 12: K1, P3; with Variegated, K8; with Lime Green, P3, K1.

Neck Shaping

K2 tog, K3; with Variegated, bind off next 6 sts in **knit**, cut Variegated; with Lime Green, K2, SSK: 4 sts **each** side.

FIRST SIDE

Row 1: K1, P3.

Row 2: K4.

Row 3: K1, P3.

Bind off all sts on First Side in **knit**.

SECOND SIDE

Row 1: With **wrong** side facing and remaining Lime Green, P3, K1.

Row 2: K4.

Row 3: P3, K1.

Bind off 3 sts in **knit**; do **not** cut yarn: one st.

Slip st onto crochet hook, ch 12; with **right** side facing, join with slip st to first st on First Side, **turn**; slip st in each ch across; finish off.

General Instructions

ABBREVIATIONS

ch(s)	chain(s)
cm	centimeters
K	knit
M1	Make One
mm	millimeters
P	purl
PSSO	pass slipped stitch over
P2SSO	pass 2 slipped stitches over
SSK	slip, slip, knit
st(s)	stitch(es)
tog	together
YO	yarn over

SYMBOLS & TERMS

★ — work instructions following ★ as many **more** times as indicated in addition to the first time.

( ) or **[ ]** — work enclosed instructions **as many** times as specified by the number immediately following **or** work all instructions in the stitch indicated **or** contains explanatory remarks.

colon (:) — the number(s) given after a colon at the end of a row denote(s) the number of stitches you should have on that row.

KNIT TERMINOLOGY		
UNITED STATES		INTERNATIONAL
gauge	=	tension
bind off	=	cast off
yarn over (YO)	=	yarn forward (yfwd) **or** yarn around needle (yrn)

BEGINNER	Projects for first-time knitters using basic knit and purl stitches. Minimal shaping.
EASY	Projects using basic stitches, repetitive stitch patterns, simple color changes, and simple shaping and finishing.
INTERMEDIATE	Projects with a variety of stitches, such as basic cables and lace, simple intarsia, double-pointed needles and knitting in the round needle techniques, mid-level shaping and finishing.
EXPERIENCED	Projects using advanced techniques and stitches, such as short rows, fair isle, more intricate intarsia, cables, lace patterns, and numerous color changes.

GAUGE

The dishcloth dresses are written for medium weight 100% cotton yarn. Gauge is not of great importance; your dishcloth may be a little larger or smaller without changing the overall effect.

KNITTING NEEDLES		
UNITED STATES	ENGLISH U.K.	METRIC (mm)
0	13	2
1	12	2.25
2	11	2.75
3	10	3.25
4	9	3.5
5	8	3.75
6	7	4
7	6	4.5
8	5	5
9	4	5.5
10	3	6
10 1/2	2	6.5
11	1	8
13	00	9
15	000	10
17	---	12.75
19	---	15
35	---	19
50	---	25

Yarn Weight Symbol & Names	LACE 0	SUPER FINE 1	FINE 2	LIGHT 3	MEDIUM 4	BULKY 5	SUPER BULKY 6	JUMBO 7
Type of Yarns in Category	Fingering, size 10 crochet thread	Sock, Fingering, Baby	Sport, Baby	DK, Light Worsted	Worsted, Afghan, Aran	Chunky, Craft, Rug	Super Bulky, Roving	Jumbo, Roving
Knit Gauge Ranges in Stockinette St to 4" (10 cm)	33-40 sts**	27-32 sts	23-26 sts	21-24 sts	16-20 sts	12-15 sts	7-11 sts	6 sts and fewer
Advised Needle Size Range	000 to 1	1 to 3	3 to 5	5 to 7	7 to 9	9 to11	11 to 17	17 and larger

* GUIDELINES ONLY: The chart above reflects the most commonly used gauges and needle sizes for specific yarn categories.

** Lace weight yarns are usually knitted on larger needles to create lacy openwork patterns. Accordingly, a gauge range is difficult to determine. Always follow the gauge stated in your pattern.

INCREASES

Knit Increase

Knit the next stitch but do **not** slip the old stitch off the left needle *(Fig. 1a)*. Insert the right needle into the back loop of the **same** stitch and knit it *(Fig. 1b)*, then slip the old stitch off the left needle.

Fig. 2

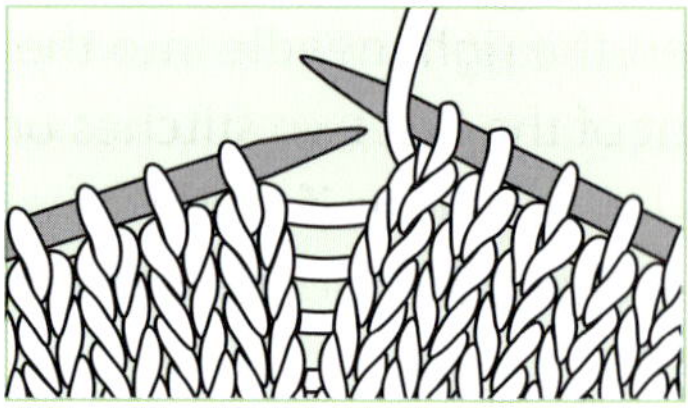

Fig. 1a

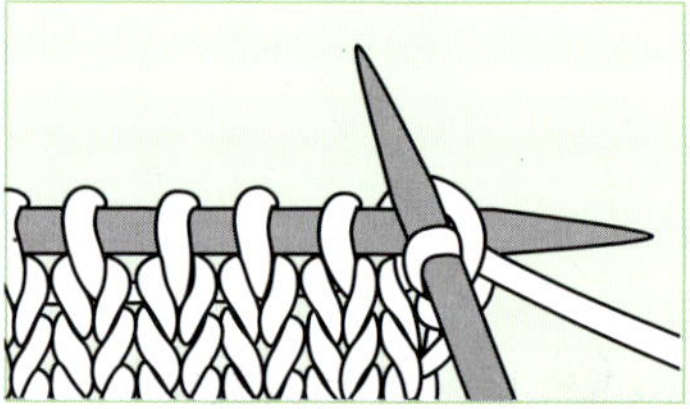

Make One *(abbreviated M1)*

Insert the left needle under the horizontal strand between the stitches from the **front** *(Fig. 3a)*. Then knit into the **back** of the strand *(Fig. 3b)*.

Fig. 1b

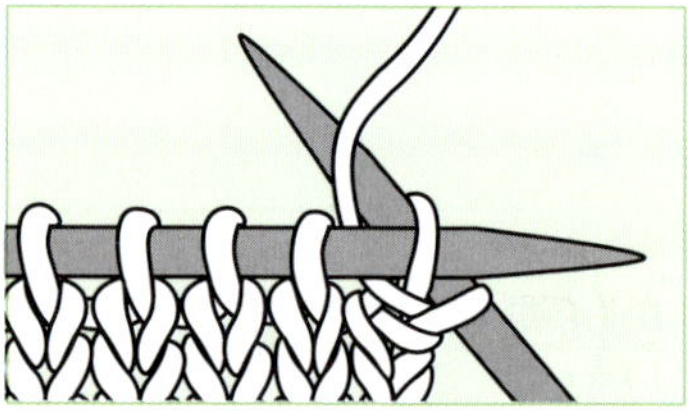

Fig. 3a

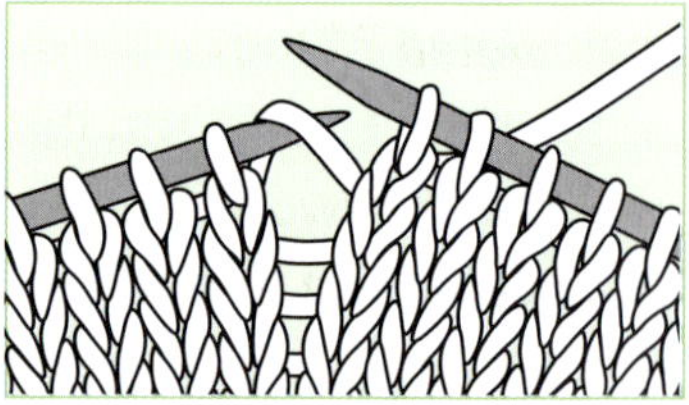

Fig. 3b

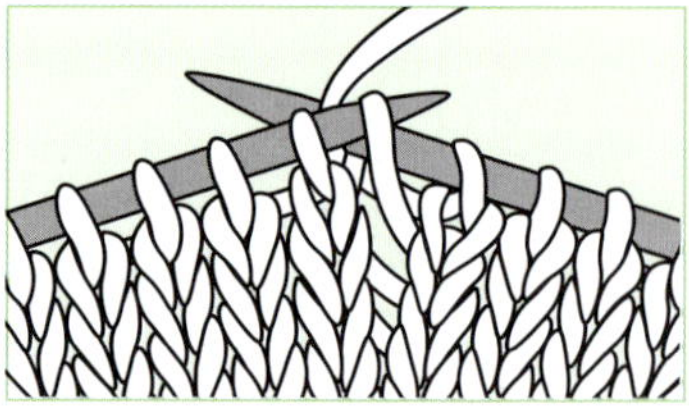

Yarn Over *(abbreviated YO)*

Bring the yarn forward **between** the needles, then back **over** the top of the right needle, so that it is now in position to knit the next stitch *(Fig. 2)*.

DECREASES

Knit 2 together

(abbreviated K2 tog)

Insert the right needle into the **front** of the first two stitches on the left needle as if to **knit** *(Fig. 4)*, then **knit** them together as if they were one stitch.

Fig. 4

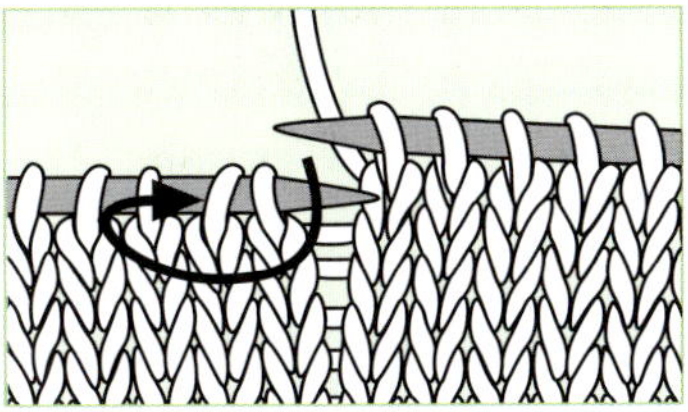

Purl 2 Together

(abbreviated P2 tog)

Insert the right needle into the **front** of the first two stitches on the left needle as if to **purl** *(Fig. 5)*, then **purl** them together as if they were one stitch.

Fig. 5

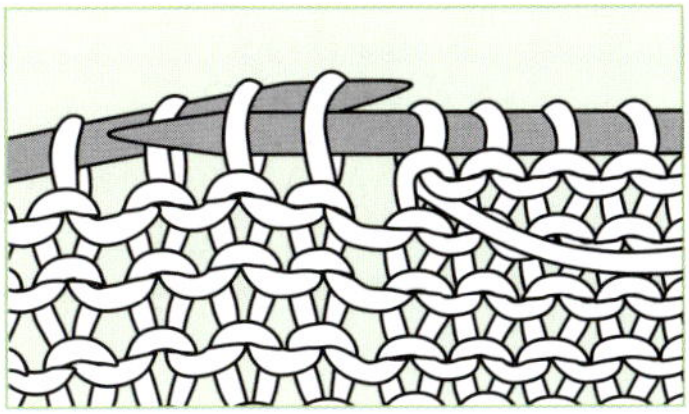

Slip, Slip, Knit

(abbreviated SSK)

With yarn in back of work, separately slip two stitches as if to **knit** *(Fig. 6a)*. Insert the **left** needle into the **front** of both slipped stitches *(Fig. 6b)* and knit them together as if they were one stitch *(Fig. 6c)*.

Fig. 6a

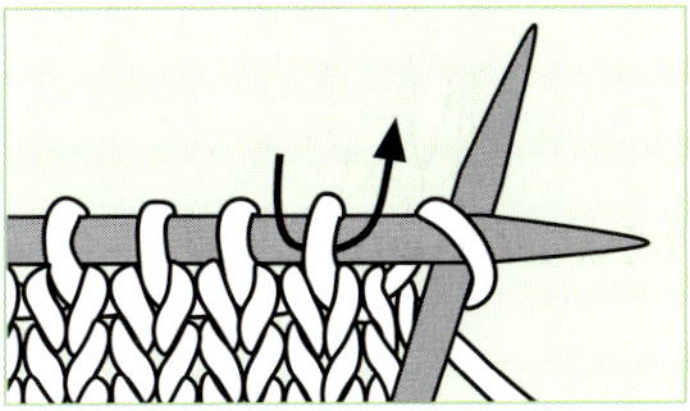

Fig. 6b

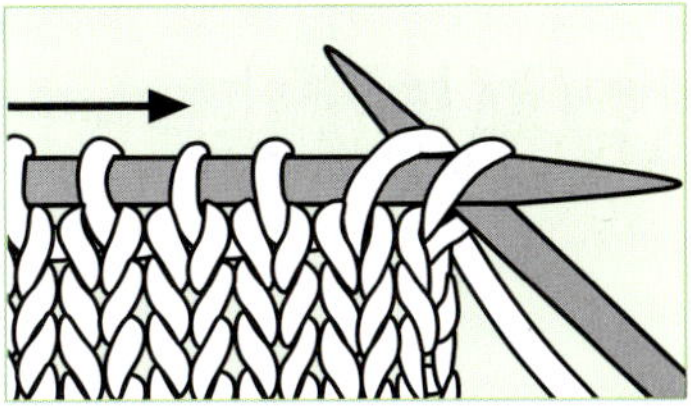

Fig. 6c

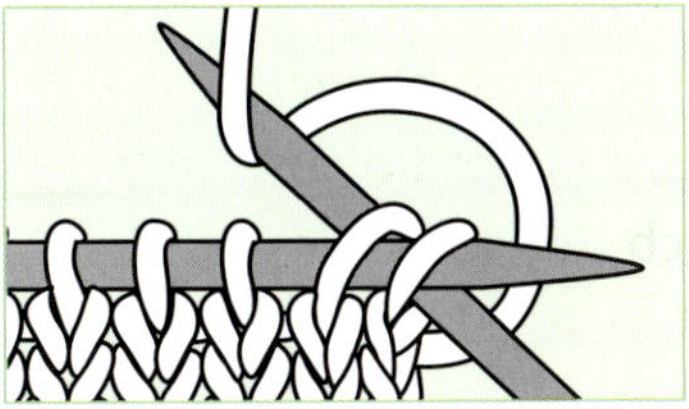

Slip 1, Knit 1, Pass Slipped Stitch Over

(abbreviated slip 1, K1, PSSO)

Slip one stitch as if to **knit** *(Fig. 7a)*. Knit the next stitch. With the left needle, bring the slipped stitch over the knit stitch *(Fig. 7b)* and off the needle.

Fig. 7a

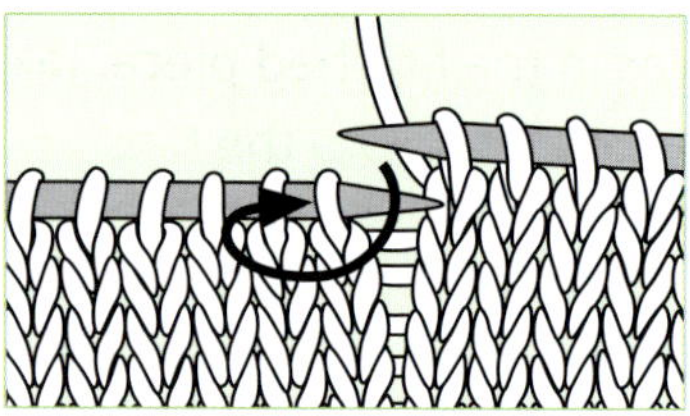

Fig. 7b

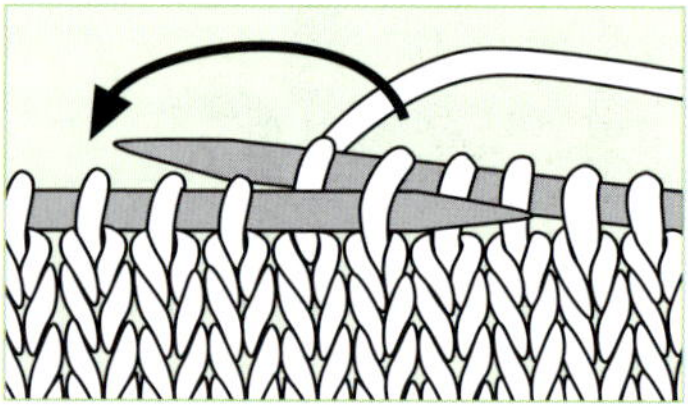

Slip 1, Knit 2 Together, Pass Slipped Stitch Over

(abbreviated slip 1, K2 tog, PSSO)

Slip one stitch as if to **knit** *(Fig. 7a)*, then knit the next two stitches together *(Fig. 4, page 27)*. With the left needle, bring the slipped stitch over the stitch just made *(Fig. 8)* and off the needle.

Fig. 8

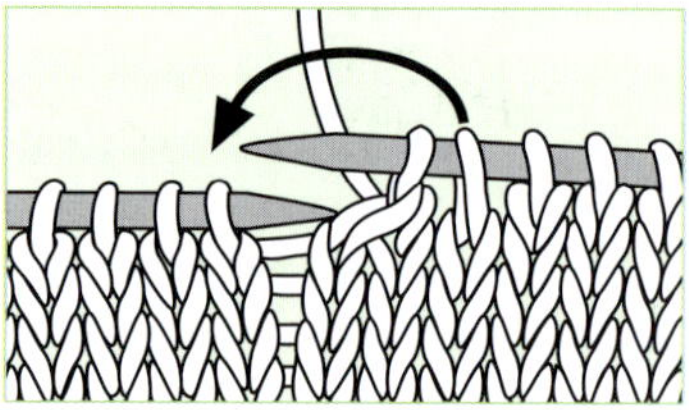

Slip 2 Together, Knit 1, Pass 2 Slipped Stitches Over *(abbreviated slip 2 tog, K1, P2SSO)*

Slip two stitches together as if to **knit** *(Fig. 9a)*. Knit the next stitch. With the left needle, bring the 2 slipped stitches over the knit stitch and off the needle *(Fig. 9b)*.

Fig. 9a

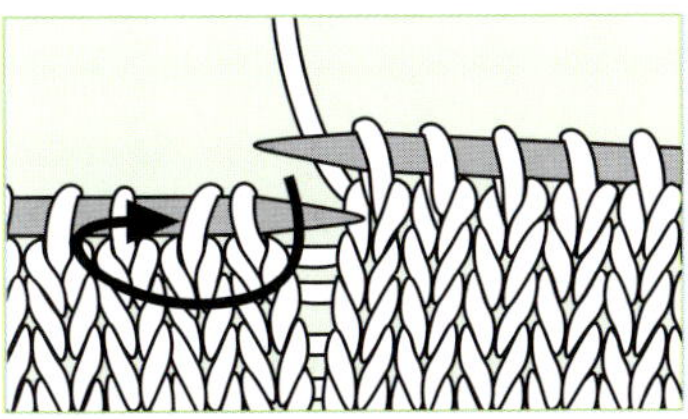

Fig. 9b

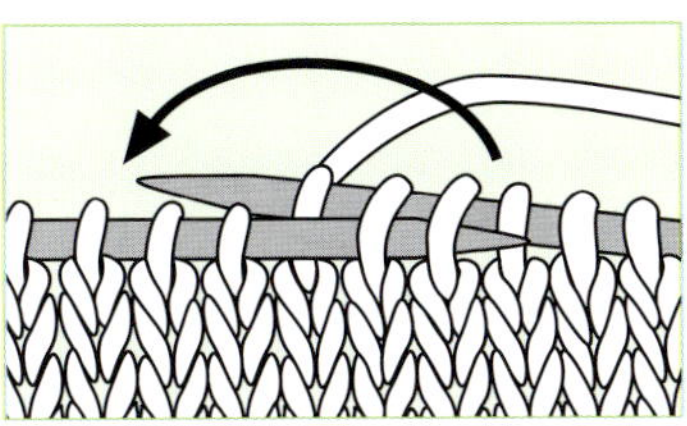

CHANGING COLORS

Wind the specified amount of yarn indicated in the instructions into a separate ball. Always keep the unused colors on the **wrong** side of the work. When changing colors, always pick up the new color yarn from **beneath** the dropped yarn and keep the color which has just been worked to the left *(Fig. 10)*. This will prevent holes in the finished piece. Take extra care to keep the tension even.

Fig. 10

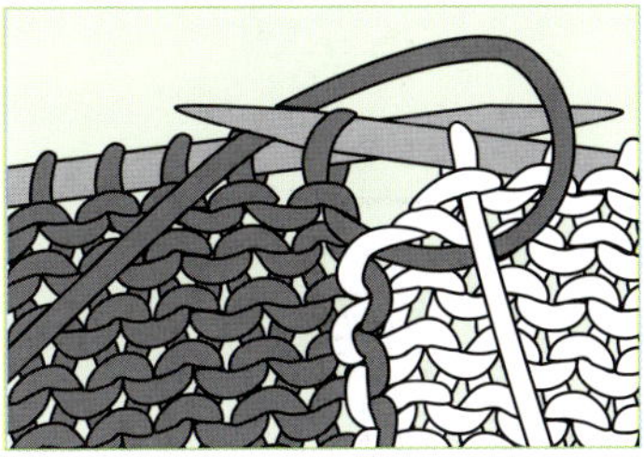

BASIC CROCHET STITCHES

Chain *(abbreviated ch)*

With the stitch on crochet hook, ★ bring the yarn over the hook from **back** to **front**, catching the yarn with the hook and turning the hook slightly toward you to keep the yarn from slipping off, draw the yarn through the stitch *(Fig. 11)*; repeat from ★ for the required number of chains.

Fig. 11

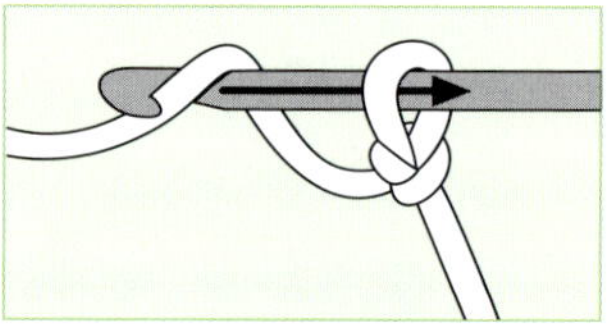

Working Into A Chain

Insert the hook under the top two strands of each chain *(Fig. 12)*.

Fig. 12

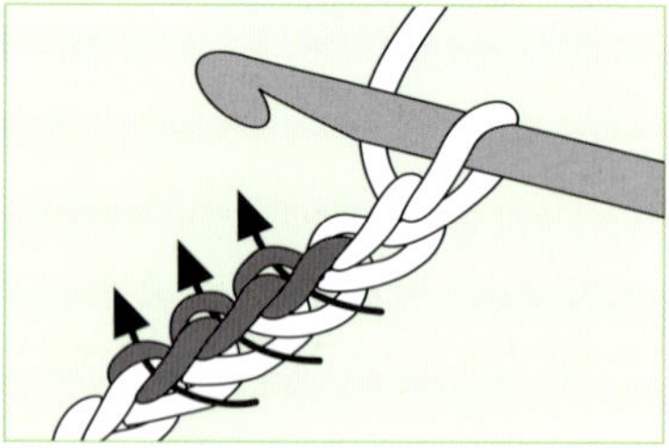

Slip Stitch *(abbreviated slip st)*

Insert the hook in stitch indicated, bring the yarn over the hook and draw through stitch and through loop on hook (slip st made, *Fig. 13)*.

Fig. 13

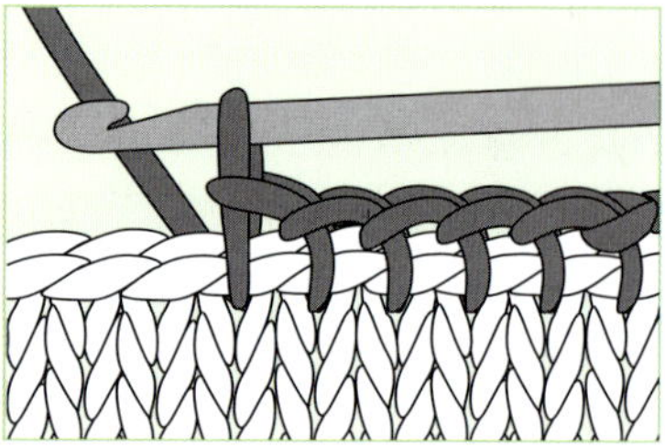

Yarn Information

The dishcloth dresses in this book were made using Lily® Sugar 'n Cream®, a 100% cotton Medium Weight Yarn. Any Medium Weight Yarn may be used. It is best to refer to the yardage/meters to determine how many balls or skeins to purchase.

For your convenience, listed below are the specific colors used to create our photography models. Because yarn manufacturers make frequent changes in their product lines, you may sometimes find it necessary to use a substitute yarn or to search for the discontinued product at alternate suppliers (locally or online).

Sunday
Brunch Dress
#01201 Seabreeze

Monday
Shopping Spree Dress
#01740 Hot Pink

Tuesday
Lunch With Friends Dress
#00073 Sunshine

Wednesday
At The Museum Dress
#01215 Robin's Egg

Thursday
Off To The Spa Dress
#00042 Tea Rose

Friday
Dinner Date Dress
#01317 Hot Purple

Saturday
At The Beach Dress
Variegated - #02746 Summer Prints
Lime Green - #01712 Hot Green

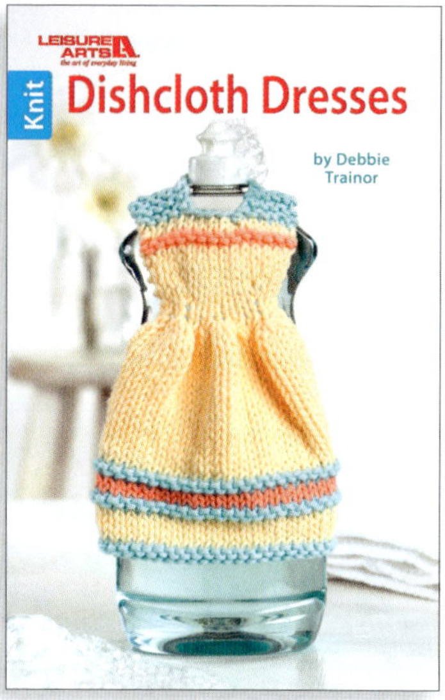

Add more fun to your kitchen counter with the 12 additional designs in *Dishcloth Dresses* (Leisure Arts Book #75428).

We have made every effort to ensure that these instructions are accurate and complete. We cannot, however, be responsible for human error, typographical mistakes, or variations in individual work.

Production Team: Instructional/Technical Writer - Linda A. Daley; Editorial Writer - Susan Frantz Wiles; Senior Graphic Artist - Lora Puls; Graphic Artist - Victoria Temple; Photo Stylist - Lori Wenger; and Photographer - Jason Masters.